SPOTLIGHT ON CIVIC ACTION

UNDERSTANDING U.S. ELECTIONS AND THE ELECTORAL COLLEGE

GRACE HOUSER

PowerKiDS press.

NEW YORK

Published in 2018 by The Rosen Publishing Group, Inc.
29 East 21st Street, New York, NY 10010

Editor: Melissa Raé Shofner
Book Design: Michael Flynn
Interior Layout: Reann Nye

Cataloging-in-Publication Data

Names: Houser, Grace.
Title: Understanding U.S. elections and the Electoral College / Grace Houser.
Description: New York : PowerKids Press, 2018. | Series: Spotlight on civic action | Includes index.
Identifiers: ISBN 9781538327968 (pbk.) | ISBN 9781508164012 (library bound) | ISBN 9781538328088 (6 pack)
Subjects: LCSH: Voting--United States--Juvenile literature. | Elections--United States--Juvenile literature. | Political participation--United States--Juvenile literature. | Electoral college--United States--Juvenile literature.
Classification: LCC JK1978.H68 2018 | DDC 324.973--dc23

Manufactured in China

CONTENTS

CHAPTER ONE

A CIVIC DUTY

The right to have a say in government has been important to U.S. citizens from the very beginning. As colonists, they wanted to be heard in the British government. After winning independence, colonial leaders established the United States as a republic. In this type of government, citizens vote for people to represent them in government.

Voting is the act of choosing a candidate in an election. Taking part in elections is one way citizens can take part in government. Elections give citizens a say in who represents them at the local, state, and national levels of government. They're voting in support of ideas candidates have included in their **platforms**. Being part of the election process is a **civic** duty. You're taking a stand for what you believe in and supporting the U.S. Constitution.

In the United States, citzens vote for national representatives who serve in Congress, which is made up of the House of Representatives and the Senate. This painting by Samuel F. B. Morse shows the House of Representatives in 1822.

CHAPTER TWO

WHO CAN VOTE?

Voting hasn't always been something every adult citizen could do. At the time the Declaration of Independence was signed, only property owners—most of whom were white men—could vote. Once the U.S. Constitution was adopted, the states were in charge of deciding who would be allowed to vote. It remained mostly white male landowners. During the mid-1800s, the vote was expanded to all white men. In 1869, African American men gained the right to vote. Women were allowed the right to vote in 1920.

Today, U.S. citizens age 18 or older can vote in many governmental elections. However, U.S. citizens who live in U.S. territories, such as Guam and Puerto Rico, can't vote in presidential elections. Some states don't allow people who have committed certain types of crimes to vote.

HOUSE OF REPRESENTATIVES

AGE: MUST BE 25 OR OLDER

LENGTH OF CITIZENSHIP: AT LEAST 7 YEARS

LENGTH OF TERM: 2 YEARS

SENATE

AGE: MUST BE 30 OR OLDER

LENGTH OF CITIZENSHIP: AT LEAST 9 YEARS

LENGTH OF TERM: 6 YEARS

PRESIDENT

AGE: MUST BE 35 OR OLDER

LENGTH OF CITIZENSHIP: SINCE BIRTH; MUST HAVE LIVED IN THE UNITED STATES FOR AT LEAST 14 YEARS

LENGTH OF TERM: 4 YEARS

The Constitution states who can run in elections for both houses of Congress and for president. Towns and states often have laws about who can run for office, too.

CHAPTER THREE

HOW ELECTIONS WORK

Each year, there are many elections all over the country. Voters head to the **polls** to choose local leaders, such as mayors and county **executives**. Members of state **legislatures** are also elected officials. Where you live will determine for whom you can vote, as some state offices only represent a certain area called a district. The state governor is also elected to office. Local and state elections can happen at any time during the year.

Most U.S. elections are decided by popular vote. Popular vote is the sum of votes cast in a political race. The candidate who wins the most votes is elected into office. Bill de Blasio won 73 percent of the popular vote in the 2013 election for New York City mayor.

Before some general elections, there are primary elections. In a primary, voters choose from a number of candidates who could represent a political party in the general election. Some primaries are "open," meaning anyone can vote in them. Others are "closed," which means only members of that political party can vote in them.

CHAPTER FOUR

RUNNING FOR CONGRESS

The process to elect members of Congress is similar to that of local and state elections. There is often a primary election to decide what candidate will run for each political party. Then, in a general election, popular vote determines who will win each seat in Congress. Members of the House of Representatives, like some in state legislatures, are elected by the **constituency** in their district. All registered voters in a state have a chance to vote for their senators.

House representatives serve two-year terms. Senators serve six-year terms. Sometimes a congressperson will leave a **vacant** seat because of death, a new position, or **resignation**. In many states, a special election is held to fill the seat. In other states, however, the governor chooses a person to take the office without an election.

The two major political parties in the United States are the Democrats and the Republicans. However, some members of Congress, such as Senator Bernie Sanders, aren't part of those parties and are called independents.

CHAPTER FIVE

THE ROAD TO THE PRESIDENCY

Every four years, the United States holds an election for president. Unlike the other elections around the nation, this election isn't decided by popular vote. The Electoral College, established by the U.S. Constitution, is the body through which the president is elected.

First, however, candidates have to get on the **ballot**. Candidates must officially declare they're running for

The Iowa caucuses are the first primary or caucus to occur during a presidential election year. In late October 2016, Democratic presidential nominee Hillary Clinton held a campaign rally in Cedar Rapids, Iowa.

president. They usually do this more than a year before the election. From January to June of an election year, states and political parties have to decide whom they want to support for the party's nomination. Some states hold primaries. Others allow political parties to hold special meetings called caucuses. At a caucus, residents can stand with others who support the same candidate and cast a paper ballot.

CHAPTER SIX

THE OFFICIAL NOMINATION

Once the votes in primaries and caucuses have been counted, political parties award candidates for president a number of delegates. Delegates represent their fellow voters at the political party **conventions** that occur during the summer before a presidential election. The candidate with the most delegates wins their party's official nomination at the national convention. Even small political parties, such as the Libertarian Party, have conventions during which they choose a presidential candidate. Today, the most visible candidates in the presidential election are from the Republican and Democratic Parties.

The official nominees spend the next few months campaigning all across the country. They give speeches, answer questions, and take part in **debates** to win over voters before they head to the polls on the Tuesday after the first Monday in November.

President Donald Trump earned the Republican nomination for president in 2016 by winning more than enough delegates through state primaries and caucuses.

CHAPTER SEVEN

CASTING A VOTE

In most elections, including the one for president, voters head to their local polling place, or a building at which they can cast their votes. These are often community centers, churches, fire halls, and other places with lots of space to set up private voting areas. Depending on where you live, how your vote is cast will be different. Some states still have paper ballots that are

POLLING PLACE
投票站 CASILLA ELECTORAL
投票所 LUGAR NG BOTOHAN
투표소 PHÒNG PHIẾU

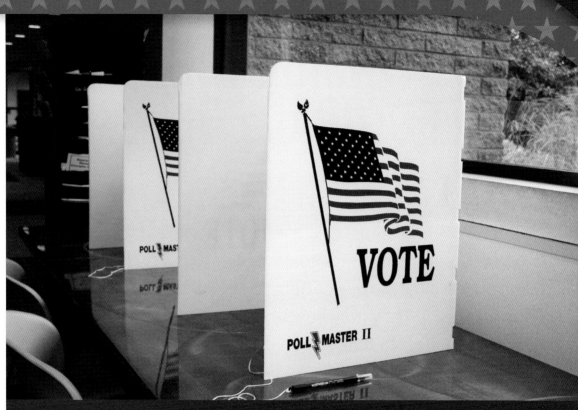

It can be hard to make time to vote, but it's an important part of making the U.S. government work for its citizens.

filled in using a pencil. Others have computerized or online voting. All votes are cast in secret.

Citizens serving in the military, attending college in another state, or living in other countries can often still vote. They can vote by mailing in a ballot. This is called absentee voting, and the rules about who can do it and how they do it are different in each state.

CHAPTER EIGHT

INSIDE THE ELECTORAL COLLEGE

After citizens' ballots are cast, the Electoral College is ready to do its job. The Electoral College is made up of electors. When voters cast a vote for president, they're actually voting for these electors. Electors may be leaders within political parties or people who work in the state government. They may have a connection to one of the presidential candidates. Each candidate has their own set of electors.

It may seem like a confusing system, but the Electoral College comes from the Founding Fathers. Some of them wanted the president to be elected by popular vote. Others didn't trust the average citizen to elect the president and wanted Congress to choose the president. The Electoral College was included in the U.S. Constitution as a compromise between these two ideas.

STATE OF MICHIGAN

MICHIGAN PRESIDENTIAL ELECTOR
OFFICIAL BALLOT FOR PRESIDENT OF
THE UNITED STATES

I hereby cast my vote for Donald J. Trump
for President of the United States.

Signed _____

Hank Fuhs

The Constitution doesn't say who can be an elector. States have different rules and ways of choosing people for these positions.

CHAPTER NINE

KNOW THE NUMBERS

Each state is **allotted** a number of electors equal to its number of House representatives and senators. Washington, D.C., also has three electors. The Electoral College is made up of 538 electors who each cast one electoral vote. Washington, D.C., and 48 states award all their electoral votes to one candidate who wins the majority of the popular vote. Maine and Nebraska divide theirs between candidates based on how many popular votes they receive.

Often, it's clear on voting day who will become president. The Electoral College doesn't vote for president until the first Monday after the second Wednesday in December—that's when a candidate truly wins the election. The U.S. Constitution doesn't say that electors must vote with the popular vote of their state, but it's very rare for electors to cast a vote against their state's decision.

U.S. ELECTORAL MAP,
2016 PRESIDENTIAL ELECTION

State	Votes
WA	12
OR	7
CA	55
NV	6
ID	4
MT	3
WY	3
UT	6
AZ	11
CO	9
NM	5
ND	3
SD	3
NE	5
KS	6
OK	7
TX	38
MN	10
IA	6
MO	10
AR	6
LA	8
WI	10
IL	20
MI	16
IN	11
OH	18
KY	8
TN	11
MS	6
AL	9
GA	16
WV	5
VA	13
NC	15
SC	9
FL	29
PA	20
NY	29
VT	3
NH	4
ME	3 (1)
MA	11
RI	4
CT	7
NJ	14
DE	3
MD	10
DC	3
AK	3
HI	4

This map shows how the Electoral College voted in the 2016 U.S. presidential election. The red states represent electoral votes for the Republican candidate and the blue states represent electoral votes for the Democratic candidate.

CHAPTER TEN

WINNING THE ELECTORAL COLLEGE

In order to win the presidency, a candidate must receive more than half the electoral votes, or at least 270. The Constitution provides a solution if one candidate doesn't earn a majority of electoral votes, though that's only happened one time in U.S. history. In this case, the members of the House of Representatives vote for president. That's how John Quincy Adams was elected president in 1824.

With the Electoral College, it's possible for a candidate to win enough electoral votes to become president even if they lose the popular vote. That's only happened five times in history. Most recently, this happened during the 2016 presidential election. Democrat Hillary Clinton won the popular vote. However, she lost the presidency to Republican Donald Trump, who won the majority of electoral votes.

The electoral votes are officially counted at a joint session of Congress on January 6 after the Electoral College votes. The vice president reads the result. In this image from January 6, 2017, House Speaker Paul Ryan reacts to Vice President Joe Biden's announcement that Donald Trump received the most electoral votes.

CHAPTER ELEVEN

OUTDATED OR TIMELESS?

Many people don't fully understand how the Electoral College works. That's just one reason it's often criticized today.

Some critics believe that each registered voter should get one vote and that all people's votes should be equal. In the Electoral College system, states with smaller populations may have more electors per person than states with bigger populations. In addition, the winner-take-all awarding of electoral votes overlooks candidates

Some people don't like that the Electoral College winner-take-all system doesn't allow smaller political parties to make much of a difference in who earns electoral votes.

who win a significant amount—but not a majority—of the popular vote in a state.

The only way to change the Electoral College system of electing the president is to amend, or change, the Constitution. In fact, more than 700 amendments to change the Electoral College have been proposed. None have gained enough support. This is probably because the winner of the Electoral College has most often won the popular vote, too.

ELECTION ISSUES TODAY

Even though Congress has passed laws designed to end voter **discrimination**, it remains an issue today. Voter identification (ID) laws in some states make it harder for some people to vote. It can be difficult to obtain the ID these laws require.

Issues of discrimination have become worse since a 2013 Supreme Court ruling weakened the Voting Rights Act. The act was passed in 1965 and has been renewed many times. It once made some states, especially in the South, clear new voting laws with the federal justice department. This was meant to reduce historical discrimination in those areas.

The money used to run in an election is an issue of concern, too. The vast amounts people and groups give to candidates can seem troubling. Many believe these contributions buy influence on the candidate's platform and, perhaps, their actions in office.

It costs millions of dollars to run for Congress. This means wealthier people have an easier time running in an election. The Center for Responsive Politics (CRP) estimated that 47 percent of Congress members were millionaires in 2010. The CRP estimated that Nancy Pelosi, shown here, was the seventh wealthiest member of Congress in 2014.

CHAPTER THIRTEEN

CHOOSING HOW TO VOTE

As a voter, you should spend some time gathering information about each candidate. Think about what's important to you in a candidate. If it's a local election, for example, you might look for someone who supports cleaning up parks. Then, read newspaper or online articles about each candidate's background. Check out their website or social media accounts to see what they've included in their platform. Some elections, such as those for U.S.

Voters play a huge part in how elections work in the United States. Many people take time to pass out information about candidates they support.

president, have debates you can watch. In debates, major candidates speak about the same topics so voters can see how they match up.

Sometimes you might find a candidate you agree with completely. You can show them even more support by putting a sign supporting them on your lawn or telling friends about them. You might help them win over more voters.

CHAPTER FOURTEEN

YOU'RE A VOTER!

You may not be old enough to vote yet, but you can still become involved in an election. When a local, state, or national election occurs, take the time to get to know the candidates and the issues they're talking about the best you can. Ask your teachers lots of questions so you can start to understand voter issues before you need to make the tough choices at your polling place. Some candidates run for office for several terms in a row, so by the time you're ready to vote, they might still be up for reelection.

You may be able to take part in an election process at your school. Many schools have a student council, and clubs often elect leaders. You might be able to see the popular vote process up close and personal.

GLOSSARY

allot (uh-LOT) To assign a share of something.

ballot (BAA-lut) A sheet of paper listing candidates' names, used for voting.

civic (SIH-vik) Relating to the affairs and concerns of the community in which a person lives.

constituency (kuhn-STICH-went-see) The people who live and vote in an area.

convention (kuhn-VEN-shun) A gathering of people who have a common interest or purpose.

debate (dih-BAYT) An argument or public discussion.

discrimination (dis-krih-muh-NAY-shun) Different—usually unfair—treatment based on factors such as a person's race, age, religion, or gender.

executive (eg-ZEK-yoo-tiv) Someone who runs a company or government.

legislature (LEH-jis-lay-chur) A lawmaking body.

platform (PLAT-form) A plan of action or statement of beliefs.

poll (POHL) The place where votes are cast and recorded.

resignation (reh-zig-NAY-shun) The act of quitting or surrendering.

vacant (VAY-kuhnt) Empty.

INDEX

PRIMARY SOURCE LIST

Page 5
The House of Representatives. Painting. Samuel F. B. Morse. ca. 1822–1823. Now held at the National Gallery of Art, Washington, D.C.

Page 9
Mayor Bill de Blasio during his second annual state of the city address. Photograph. Baruch College, New York City. February 3, 2015. From Shutterstock.com.

Page 15
President Donald Trump delivering remarks on U.S.–Cuba relations in Miami, FL. Photograph. Joe Raedle. June 16, 2017. From Getty Images.

WEBSITES

Due to the changing nature of Internet links, PowerKids Press has developed an online list of websites related to the subject of this book. This site is updated regularly. Please use this link to access the list: www.powerkidslinks.com/sociv/elec